LEGENDS OF WARFARE
GROUND

M24 Chaffee, Vol. 1
American Light Tank in World War II, Korea, and Vietnam

DAVID DOYLE

SCHIFFER MILITARY
4880 Lower Valley Road • Atglen, PA 19310

Designed by Justin Watkinson
Technical Layout by Jack Chappell
Type set in Impact/Minion Pro/Univers LT Std

ISBN: 978-0-7643-5859-3
Printed in China

Published by Schiffer Publishing, Ltd.
4880 Lower Valley Road
Atglen, PA 19310
Phone: (610) 593-1777; Fax: (610) 593-2002
E-mail: Info@schifferbooks.com
www.schifferbooks.com

For our complete selection of fine books on this and related subjects, please visit our website at www.schifferbooks.com. You may also write for a free catalog.

Schiffer Publishing's titles are available at special discounts for bulk purchases for sales promotions or premiums. Special editions, including personalized covers, corporate imprints, and excerpts, can be created in large quantities for special needs. For more information, contact the publisher.

We are always looking for people to write books on new and related subjects. If you have an idea for a book, please contact us at proposals@schifferbooks.com.

Acknowledgments

As with all of my projects, this book would not have been possible without the generous help of many friends. Instrumental to the completion of this book were Tom Kailbourn, Allan Cors, Marc Sehring, Brent Mullins, Sean Hert, Joe DeMarco, Eli Geher, the late Dave Harper, and Scott Taylor, as well as the archivists at General Motors, the staff and volunteers at the Patton Museum, the staff at the National Archives, and the staff at the US Veteran's Memorial Museum in Huntsville, Alabama. Most importantly, I am blessed to have the help and support of my wife, Denise, for which I am eternally grateful.

Contents

Introduction

Owing to the shortcomings of the 37 mm gun in the M3- and M5-series light tanks, the Army sought a new light tank with a more potent 75 mm main gun powered by a twin Cadillac sixteen-cylinder engine in 1943. The new vehicle, designated the Light Tank T24, was authorized for development by Cadillac Motor Car Division of General Motors on April 29, 1943. Following the production of a wooden mockup of the T24 in May 1943, Chrysler completed two pilot tanks; this photo almost certainly shows one of those pilots. The prominent, octagonal access door on the glacis for the differential would remain a feature throughout M24 production. *General Motors LLC*

While the twin Cadillac power plant of the M5A1 Stuart light tanks had proven sound and reliable, as had the Hydramatic transmission, combat in North Africa had proven that the 37 mm gun of the M5-series tank, and its predecessor the M3-series tank, was not adequate. In March 1943, efforts began to incorporate the 75 mm gun M3 into a light tank utilizing the M5A1 drivetrain. Soon, in an effort to reduce the vehicle weight, attention turned to substituting the T13E1 75 mm gun, which had been developed for use in the B-25H Mitchell medium bomber. This thin-walled cannon was adapted for vehicle use through the use of a short recoil mechanism. The result was designated the T90 combination gun mount and was incorporated into the M6 75 mm gun (as the T13E1 had been subsequently designated), the T33 recoil mechanism, a T92 sight, and a .30-caliber coaxial machine gun.

The Ordnance Department selected Cadillac as the prime contractor for the new tank. Ordnance and Cadillac engineers opted to utilize torsion bar suspension for the new vehicle, and a chassis was designed incorporating five pairs of road wheels per side. Atop the chassis was placed a turret with a 60-inch-diameter ring. Because of problems in the field with the automatic transfer case used in the M5, a manual transfer unit was developed for the new vehicle. The new design was designated T24 per Ordnance Committee Minutes (OCM) 21446 of September 2, 1943.

The decision to use the twin Cadillac V-8 power plant and torsion bar suspension proved a sound one. The reliable T24 power train and suspension were incorporated into the numerous variants of the Chaffee, including the M19, M37, and M41 motor carriages, which are covered in the second volume of this series of books.

The first T24 pilot arrived at Aberdeen Proving Ground, Maryland, for testing on October 15, 1943. This vehicle bore the stencil on the forward part of the upper hull, "T-24-1 / EXP. PILOT," with "EXP" standing for experimental. The main gun chosen for this tank was the 75 mm Gun T13E1 on the short-recoil Mount T90; in production M24s this weapon would be standardized as the 75 mm Gun M6 in Mount M64. *General Motors LLC*

The turret of the Light Tank T24 was designed from scratch, and the hull was an adaptation of an existing design for a self-propelled artillery piece. The turret was larger and more commodious than that of the Light Tank M5A1, necessitating a larger turret ring. As seen in an elevated photo of one of the pilot T24s, the loader's hatch on the right side of the turret had a bifolding door that folded forward. To the front of that hatch was a smoke mortar. The commander's and gunner's hatch on the left side of the roof had a single door with a rotating periscope. To the front of that hatch was another rotating periscope for the commander, as well as a ventilator hood. On the front left corner of the roof was the gunner's periscope, on a fixed mount. The engine exhausts are visible on the engine deck just aft of the fuel-filler caps.
General Motors LLC

The first pilot T24 is viewed from the right rear. A storage box was mounted on the rear of the turret bustle, and a bin for storing a tarpaulin was on the rear of the hull. Straps, with the ends neatly rolled up for tying down equipment, are on the rear of the fender and on the center part of the engine deck. *General Motors LLC*

T24 pilot 1 is observed from the left rear at Aberdeen Proving Ground on October 21, 1943. The suspension utilized torsion bars; there were five dual bogie wheels on each side with 25.5-by-4.5-inch rubber tires. The tracks were the T72 single-pin type, 16 inches wide. For vehicle defense, a Browning M2 HB .50-caliber machine gun was installed on a pedestal mount on the rear of the turret roof. *Patton Museum*

A Light Tank T24 pilot is seen from the right side, with a measuring stick leaning against it for reference. A full set of sand skirts was provided for the T24s and production M24s. Protruding from the side of the turret is a bracket for a radio antenna. Pioneer tools are stored on the side of the upper hull. *Patton Museum*

CHAPTER 1
Production

Cadillac, in addition to being the design agency for the T24, was also the prime contractor for production and was issued a contract for 1,000 of the new tanks on September 23, 1943.

The first pilot was delivered to Aberdeen Proving Ground, Maryland, on October 15, 1943, with the second following in December. Testing uncovered a number of minor faults, all of which were corrected before series production began in April 1944 at the Cadillac plant in Detroit, Michigan.

The 1,000-tank order placed with Cadillac was increased to 1,550 tanks on December 27, 1943, and at the same time 250 duplicate vehicles were ordered from Massey-Harris. The farm equipment manufacturer would build the new tanks in their Racine, Wisconsin, facility.

On June 22, 1944, OCM 24175 recommended that the T24 be standardized as the M24. The vehicle was named Chaffee, recognizing Maj. Gen. Adna R. Chaffee, the first commander of the Armored Force.

While various minor changes were made during the production of the tanks, the most noticeable was the addition of adapters to allow the installation of flotation tanks. This was the result of efforts to adapt the tank to being an amphibious vehicle. With testing being somewhat successful, Cadillac began installing the adapters on the rear of the tank with serial number 713, while the front adapters did not begin to be installed until serial number 1101. Massey-Harris began including the adapters in both locations at tank serial number 250.

While ultimately 10,318 Chaffees were ordered by the US Army, the war ended before the orders were completed. As seen in the table on page 25, Cadillac had been contracted for 7,926 vehicles, and 2,392 were contracted from Massey-Harris. However, due to the end of the war, in August 1945, production at Massey-Harris ended after 1,139 tanks and at Cadillac after 3,592 of the vehicles. The last Massey-Harris registration number was 30142577, while the final Cadillac registration number was 30137761.

After the testing of the two pilot T24s and the implementation of modifications to the vehicle to correct deficiencies, the Light Tank T24 entered production at the Cadillac Division of General Motors in April 1944. In July of that year, Massey-Harris also began producing the T24, which during that month was standardized as the Light Tank M24. Shown here during evaluations at Aberdeen Proving Ground on June 23, 1944, is the second T24. *National Archives*

The second T24 is viewed from the right side at Aberdeen. On the right side of the 75 mm gun was a .30-caliber coaxial machine gun. Several noticeable changes had been made to the turret since the pilot T24s: a curved piece of armor was welded to the right side of the turret, to shield the .50-caliber machine gun from frontal fire when that gun was stored for travel on the turret aft of the shield; note the brackets for storing the machine gun. A pistol port had been added to the right side of the turret. And a cupola replaced the commander's hatch door on the turret roof. *National Archives*

More details of the new tripod support assembly for the .50-caliber machine gun are visible in this left-rear photo of the second production T24. The new cupola had six vision blocks as well as a periscope on a rotating mount on the cupola hatch door. A spotlight is mounted to the left of the cupola. The three track-support rollers are visible below the sand skirt. *National Archives*

The turret roof of the production vehicles, as shown on the second production T24, marked a significant change from that of the pilot T24s. The loader's bifolding hatch door on the right side gave way to a smaller, single-panel door. The commander's and gunner's hatch on the left side was replaced by a cupola with six vision blocks and a hatch door with a rotating dome incorporating a periscope. The ventilator was moved to the right of center. The engine exhausts had been moved farther back, to the front corners of the air outlet grille, and outboard of the exhausts were armored fuel-compartment vents. *National Archives*

The same vehicle depicted in the preceding photos, the second production T24, is viewed from the front at Aberdeen Proving Ground on January 2, 1945, by which time this and other production T24s had been redesignated Light Tank M24. Features apparent in this photo include the hard edge across the front of the mantlet, with the gunner's sight aperture above that edge and the coaxial machine gun under it; the bracket to the front of the driver's hatch for a detachable windshield; the horn next to the left headlight assembly; the differential access door on the glacis, with two grab handles; and the steps above the final drives. *National Archives*

A rear view of the second production M24 shows details of the tripod support assembly for the machine gun, with the travel lock engaged to the gun barrel; the taillight assemblies, nested inside protective brackets; the tarpaulin bin; the step on the left side of the rear of the hull; and the tow pintle. On the right side of the turret bustle, a .50-caliber ammunition box is stored on a bracket and secured with a strap. *National Archives*

For instructive purposes, General Motors prepared this M24 chassis with just the hull bottom, engines and drivetrain, suspension (less the idlers), and drivers' stations. In the foreground are the two generators on the rear of the twin Cadillac series 44T24 engine. On the front, or output, end of the engine are the two Hydramatic two-speed transmissions, which feed output to the white-colored Synchromesh transfer unit (one reverse and two forward speeds) directly to the front of the transmissions. From the transfer unit, the main driveshaft proceeds to a support bearing, between the drivers' seat backs. Thence, a short, forward driveshaft is connected to the controlled differential. *General Motors LLC*

The instructional chassis is viewed from the left rear. Running across the floor of the hull are housings, each of which contains two torsion bars. The first four bogie arms on each side of the hull pointed to the rear, while the rear bogie arms were oriented to the front. *General Motors LLC*

The twin Cadillac series 44T24 power plant, seen here from the front right, constituted two V-8 engines for a total of sixteen cylinders. Between the engines and the Synchromesh transfer unit to the right are the Hydramatic transmissions. In the fully assembled vehicle, the radiator and fan took up much of the space above the transmissions. *General Motors LLC*

The twin Cadillac series 44T24 power plant is seen from the rear, showing the belts and pulleys, the oil filters on the right sides of the engine blocks, the rears of the generators, and, above the generators, the exhaust-manifold connections. *General Motors LLC*

A view from the upper left incorporates all the components and systems as installed on the instructional chassis. Note the support bracket with two large lightening holes on the side, under the front end of the left transmission. Note the bearing between the main driveshaft and the shorter forward driveshaft. In the completed vehicle, periscope storage boxes were mounted over the forward driveshaft, acting as a shield to prevent injury to the drivers when the shafts were in operation. *General Motors LLC*

The driver's station is shown in the instructional chassis. To the front of the seats are the steering levers. Below the instrument panel is the cover for the left final driveshaft, on which are shifting instructions and a crash pad to protect the driver's knees; another crash pad is to the right of this one, on the side of the controlled differential. The large lever to the right of the seat is the transfer-unit shift control; the smaller lever to the front of the transfer shifter is the transmission-range selector. *General Motors LLC*

In a front-right view of the instructional chassis, the cover is removed from the right final driveshaft to the right side of the controlled differential. The drivers' seats were adjustable forward and aft in 1-inch increments for a total of 4 inches, and up and down in 2-inch increments for a total of 10 inches. An escape hatch is on the hull floor to the rear of the assistant driver's seat. The dark rod running along the main driveshaft is the control link for the transfer unit. *General Motors LLC*

General Data

M24	
Weight	40,500 pounds
Length	216 inches
Width	117 inches
Height	97.5 inches
Crew	5
Maximum speed	35 miles per hour
Fuel capacity	110 gallons
Range	100 miles
Electrical	24 negative ground
Hydramatic transmission speeds	4
Transfer speeds	2
Turning radius	23 feet

Armament	
Main	75 mm gun M6
Secondary	2 × .30 caliber M1919A4
Flexible	1 × .50 caliber M2HB
Ammo, main	48 rounds
Ammo, .30 caliber	3,750
Ammo, .50 caliber	440

Engine Data	
Engine make/model	2 × Cadillac 44T24
Number of cylinders	90° V-8
Displacement	349 cubic inches
Horsepower	110 @ 3,400 rpm
Torque	240 @ 1,200 rpm
Governed speed (rpm)	Not governed

Radio Equipment

The Chaffee was fitted with the SCR-508, SCR-528, or SCR-538 radio set in its turret. Command tanks also had an SCR-506 in the hull.

Light Tank M24, serial number 108, was photographed during evaluations by the Ordnance Operation, General Motors Proving Ground, on August 2, 1944. Note the bracket for the detachable windshield on the glacis to the front of the driver's hatch, the armored ventilator hood between the drivers' hatches, and the pintle for the .50-caliber machine gun mount, stored on a bracket to the rear of the pistol port. *National Archives*

In addition to Cadillac, Massey-Harris, of Racine, Wisconsin, was a producer of the Light Tank M24. In this factory view of a newly completed Light Tank M24 at Massey-Harris, the object jutting from the side of the turret, aft of the pistol port, is an ammunition box tray attached to a machine gun pintle mount. The registration number is on the side of the hull adjacent to the assistant driver's hatch but is illegible. *National Archives*

MACHINING M-24 & M-41 HULLS

First Machine - facing pads
for suspensions
Second Machine - reaming pads
for suspensions and drilling
& tapping additional holes in
openings for final drives
Third Machine - Drilling roof

On the assembly line at Massey-Harris, M24 hulls are being prepared for the installation of the suspensions. On the closest hull, a machine is facing the pads for the suspensions, while on the next hull the suspension pads are being reamed. *National Archives*

ASSEMBLY LINE

M-24 Light Tank
Turret and Gun Mount

Turrets for M24s are under assembly at Massey-Harris. They are mounted on frames that are riding on raised conveyors. On the closest turret, a plug on a retainer chain is to the front of the muzzle of the smoke-grenade mortar. *National Archives*

ASSEMBLY LINE - M-24 TANK

(Now used also for M-41)

Turrets have been installed on the first two of a line of M24 hulls at the Massey-Harris factory. Massey-Harris completed 1,139 M24s during a production run spanning from July 1944 to June 1945, compared with Cadillac's total production of 3,529 M24s from April 1944 to July 1945. *National Archives*

On May 16, 1945, Gen. Joseph "Vinegar Joe" Stilwell, formerly the US commander in the China-Burma-India theater, toured the Cadillac Motor Car Division factory. He is seen here at the center, inspecting the rear of the hull of a Light Tank M24 under construction. *Military History Institute*

White-suited mechanics and technicians are performing the final touches on M24s at the Cadillac plant. The 75 mm guns were installed by this point, but the machine guns would not be mounted until later. *General Motors LLC*

T24/M24 Registration Numbers

Cadillac

PO	Reg. No.	Reg. No. End	Serial Start	Serial End
T-11120	30112594	30113593	1	1000
T-12368	30119270	30119819	1251	1800
T-13780	30120329	30121876	1801	3348
T-13780	30137268	30139010	3709	5451
T-13780	30146429	30147787	6417	7775
T-13780	30151881	30152061	7993	8173
T-13780	30152662	30154206	8774	10318

Massey-Harris

PO	Reg. No.	Reg. No. End	Serial Start	Serial End
T-12367	30119020	30119269	1001	1250
T-13781	30121877	30122236	3349	3708
T-13781	30139011	30139425	5452	5866
T-13781	30142464	30142758	5867	6161
T-13781	30142940	30143194	6162	6416
T-13781	30152062	30152661	8174	8773
T-15782	40190683	40190899	7776	7992

Two officers and a civilian confer in front of the 10,000th light tank of all models completed by Cadillac Motor Car Division. Cadillac also had been involved in the assembly of the Light Tanks M5 and M5A1. The flat plates with six holes (three over three) atop the final drives were adapters for attaching a flotation device. Some sources erroneously refer to these features as attachment points for a dozer blade. *General Motors LLC*

A deepwater-fording kit was developed for the Light Tank M24, consisting of sealant materials and two detachable trunks: a forward one for conducting air to the engine-air inlet, and a rear one for engine exhaust and outlet air. M24 registration number 30139230 is shown here with a deep-fording kit installed during evaluations of the vehicle by the Test Operation, Army Field Forces Board No. 2. *Patton Museum*

For the air-inlet trunk, extra ductwork was necessary on the engine deck to allow for the location of the tank's air inlet under the turret bustle. A watertight cover was supplied for the 75 mm gun and mantlet. *Patton Museum*

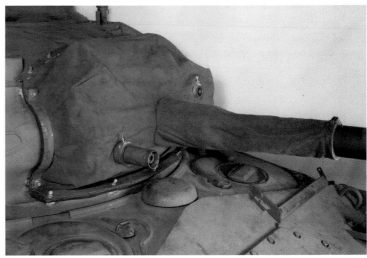

M24 registration number 30139230 is operating on a beach during tests of the deepwater-fording kit at General Motors' Milford Proving Ground, in Milford, Michigan. *Patton Museum*

The gun and mantlet cover of the M24's deep-fording kit are viewed from the right side. There were openings in the cover for the gunner's sight and the coaxial machine gun. *General Motors LLC*

A grille and doorstop, inserted in the loader's hatch of the M24 as part of the deepwater-fording kit, is viewed from the right rear during tests at the GM Milford Proving Ground. While no documentation of this arrangement has yet surfaced, it is suspected that the intent was that the engine intake air be drawn in through the turret, while the hatch door, held open by the doorstop on the grille, would provide some protection against the entry of small-arms fire, fragments, and waves. *General Motors LLC*

In a frontal view of the M24 prepared for deep fording, the headlights and the bow machine gun have been removed, and a rubber cover has been placed over the front of the bow mount. Putty-like sealant material has been packed around the horn, the hatches and periscopes, and ventilator, and duct tape has been applied over the 75 mm gun muzzle. *General Motors LLC*

The M24 with the deepwater-fording kit installed takes a swim in the pond at the Milford Proving Ground. In this photo, the loader's hatch is open all the way. *General Motors LLC*

The same M24 is seen from the right side, with the water almost up to the base of the front of the turret. The deep-fording trunks limited the turret's traverse to 310 degrees. *General Motors LLC*

In addition to the basic deep-fording kit, a flotation, or swimming, device was available for the M24. Design of the device began in mid-1944 at the Cadillac Motor Car Division, with the first unit ready for testing on October 30 of that year. M24s that were to be compatible with the flotation devices had two adapter plates added above the final drives, and two more on the rear of the hull. In this photo, the coupling for the forward part of the flotation device has been bolted to the front plates. Brackets for two pistons have been welded to the glacis. *General Motors LLC*

The rear coupling is bolted to the two adapter plates on the rear of the hull. Two jettisonable fuel tanks have been installed above the fenders. Two brackets for pistons have been welded to the upper part of the rear of the hull. Since the tracks propelled the vehicle while it was in the water, extra-wide grousers have been installed on the tracks for added effectiveness. *General Motors LLC*

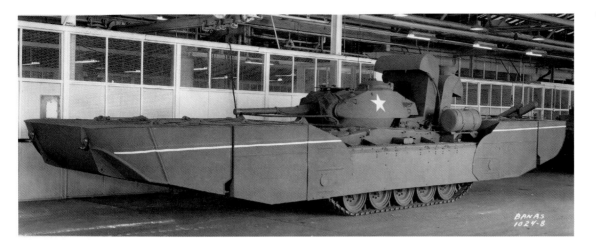

The flotation device as installed on a Light Tank M24 is viewed from the left side. The device was made up of sections. Between the forward and the rear cells, large skirts were fastened to the sides of the hull. *General Motors LLC*

The flotation device for the M24 weighed 14,000 pounds. The weight of the air intake, the outlet trunks, and the jettisonable fuel tanks as well as their contents and mounts also added to the combat weight of the vehicle. *General Motors LLC*

As seen from the left rear, the M24 flotation device had two rudders, mounted on the rear of the device. The approximate waterline is painted in white on the side. *General Motors LLC*

Only two pilot M24s fitted with flotation devices were produced. This one had a boom that has been added to the turret; here, the turret is traversed to the rear to bring the boom over the front cells of the flotation device. Although documentation on this vehicle is lacking, speculatively the boom was for the purpose of installing the flotation kit. *General Motors LLC*

The left side of the M24 fitted with the flotation device and turret-mounted boom is viewed from a closer perspective. *General Motors LLC*

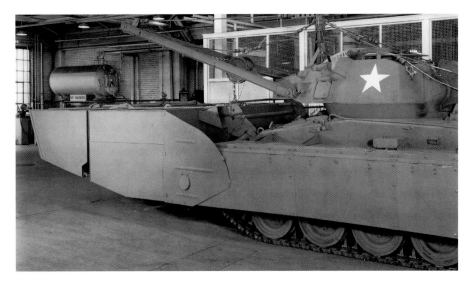

The same vehicle is viewed from the left rear, showing the rudders. Tow hooks are mounted on the horizontal tube on the stern. *General Motors LLC*

RESTRICTED

Some experiments were conducted with a bulldozer attachment on Light Tank M24, registration number 30119068. The unit was designated the Bulldozer T4 (Pilot Model) and is seen during testing at Aberdeen Proving Ground on July 24, 1944. *Patton Museum*

It was necessary to install a sizable bracket on each side of the hull to support the rear of the dozer arm. The tripod—the structure above the bulldozer blade—obviously interfered with the forward traverse of the turret when the blade was raised. *Patton Museum*

The Bulldozer T4 pilot is viewed from the right rear at Aberdeen on July 24, 1945. It is evident from the photographs that the weight of the dozer put a great amount of stress on the forward part of the suspension. *Patton Museum*

The Bulldozer T4 is shown with the blade lowered. This dozer was a revised version of the Bulldozer M1 used on the Medium Tank M4 Sherman. Above the dozer blade is the tripod, to which the front end of a hydraulic jack for operating the dozer was attached. *Patton Museum*

The M24 undergoing tests at Aberdeen with the Bulldozer T4 is viewed from above, showing the tripod from a different perspective and details of the fronts of the dozer arms. The Bulldozer T4 was found to be unsuitable because of the necessity of attaching it to the tank's suspension. Later, the Bulldozer M4 was developed for the M24, and this dozer did not rely on mounting on the suspension. *Patton Museum*

The Light Tank T24E1 pilot was equipped with a Continental R975-C4 radial engine and a Spicer automatic torque-converter transmission. American Car & Foundry Company, of Berwick, Pennsylvania, performed the conversions, using the original Light Tank T24 pilot. Testing of it began at Aberdeen Proving Ground on October 10, 1944. To accommodate the larger engine, a new, gable-shaped engine deck with extensive louvers for ventilation was fabricated. Despite the satisfactory performance of the vehicle, the T24E1 project did not advance beyond the pilot stage. *Patton Museum*

In a somewhat odd experiment, an M24 hull was stripped of its suspension, and the running gear from a German 12-ton prime mover was substituted. The rig was tested at Aberdeen Proving Ground in April 1946 but was not pursued further. *Patton Museum*

The Army Ground Forces Board No. 2 Test Operation at Fort Knox, Kentucky, experimented with Light Tank M24, registration number 30112617, with a 4.5-inch Rocket Launcher T45 mounted on each side of the turret. Each launcher fired twelve 4.5-inch Navy beach-barrage rockets. The rockets were fed by gravity and could be fired singly or in ripple fire, one after the other. Drag links from the mantlet to the launchers controlled their elevation. On the upper hull is the vehicle's nickname, "B O Plenty." *Patton Museum*

The M24 with the experimental T45 rocket launchers has just fired a salvo of 4.5-inch rockets with phosphorous payloads. *Patton Museum*

This restored and operable mid-production M24 is in the collection of Allan Cors. In addition to the original tripod mount for a .50-caliber machine gun, it has a detachable pedestal mount for a machine gun on the turret roof to the front of the hatches. This was a modification that was instituted by 1952.

The pedestal mount was to the left of center on the turret roof. It was mounted with screws on a pad with a level top that was welded to the roof. The antenna mount on the front right of the turret roof was a postwar modification.

In a left-side view of the Cors M24, note the uneven spacing of the track support rollers. On the fender above the third bogie wheel is a first-aid kit.

The Cors M24 retains the original tripod support assembly for the machine gun. On the side of the upper hull, aft of the first-aid kit, is a hood that encloses the pull handle for the interior, fixed fire-extinguisher system.

On the left fender is a holder for horizontally storing a 5-gallon liquid container. Above the upper right corner of the rear of the hull is a telephone box, which allowed infantrymen to communicate with the tank crew. The plate with the large hole in the center on each side of the rear of the hull was an adapter for attaching a flotation kit.

The Cors M24 is seen from the left side. The holder for a liquid container on the fender is evident towards the rear of the vehicle. The forward radio-antenna mount is on what formerly was the housing for the smoke-grenade mortar.

Brent Mullins of College Station, Texas, owns and restored this Light Tank M24, registration number 30120638 and serial number 2110. On the 75 mm gun barrel are replica markings for the 11th vehicle in D Company, 48th Tank Battalion, 14th Armored Division.

Fittings for storing a .50-caliber machine gun are above and aft of the pistol port on the turret.

The right sprocket is viewed from the side.

The right-sprocket assembly is viewed from the rear, showing the round lightening holes on the sprocket and the elongated ones on the drum.

Details of the front right bogie wheel are displayed. The wheel is fastened to ten studs on the hub with hex nuts. On each of the dual wheels is a 25.5-by-4.5-inch rubber tire.

There are three track-support rollers, also called track-return rollers, on each side of the hull. Each roller consists of two discs with a hub between them. The rollers were equipped with rubber tires.

Several of the bogie wheels are depicted, along with two of the roller bearings at the upper ends of the bogie support arms. The bogie wheels were buffered by aircraft-type shock absorbers and torsion bars. Bolted to the hull above each bogie wheel is a cushioned stop, to limit the upward swing of the bogie suspension arms.

The idler wheel, or track-compensating wheel, as the M24 manuals and parts catalog termed it, was designed to be adjustable so that proper track tension could be maintained. The right one is depicted.

The tracks on the Brent Mullins Light Tank M24 are the T85E1 model, which had rubber shoes with chevron grousers and required a thirteen-tooth sprocket. This photo shows another M24, equipped with the T72 cast-steel, single-pin tracks, which were the tracks originally issued to the M24s and were used during World War II.

The turret and part of the hull are observed from the right side. The pistol port is open: note the white paint on its interior, and the operating handle attached to the port. The main purpose of the port was to allow the crew to discard spent 75 mm casings without having to open the hatch doors. To the rear of the pistol port are brackets for storing a .50-caliber machine gun. On the side of the turret bustle are, *top*, a footman loop, and, *bottom*, a bracket with a footman loop on the bottom. These were for storing a .50-caliber ammo box, using a strap through the loops.

Standard features on the rear of the hull include a tarpaulin bin, a crowbar, taillight assemblies, adapters for a flotation device, and tow hooks and tow pintle. The travel lock on the tripod support for the .50-caliber machine gun is secured to the gun: specifically, to the barrel support—the perforated sleeve on the front of the gun's receiver.

The tracks on the Brent Mullins Light Tank M24 are the T85E1, which were not available until after World War II. The travel lock is engaged to the barrel of the .50-caliber machine gun.

Details of the cupola hatch door, the Browning M2 HB .50-caliber machine gun and tripod support assembly (with travel lock deployed), and the casting containing the antenna-mounting bracket are seen from the left side. Also in view is the latch for the storage compartment lid on the rear of the turret bustle.

The cupola hatch door consists of a ring on which a low dome is mounted on a ball-bearing race. This enabled rotating the dome part of the door to bring the M6 periscope on the dome to bear on the desired azimuth.

Elements in view include the storage compartment, the storage brackets for the .50-caliber machine gun and ammo box, and details of the flanges on the bottoms of the legs of the support tripod for the machine gun. Each flange is countersunk for two hex screws.

The Mullins M24's turret is observed from the right front, showing the welds, the coaxial .30-caliber machine gun barrel, the mantlet, the spotlight, and other components. Note the two lifting rings and the casting marks on the mantlet; casting marks are also present on the right front of the turret, below the housing for the smoke-grenade mortar.

The M24 restored and owned by Brent Mullins is advancing across a field toward dragon's teeth: concrete antitank obstacles replicating those that the Germans used extensively along their Siegfried Line.

The M24 is shown in closer detail as it maneuvers near the dragon's teeth.

The Mullins Light Tank M24 heads back to a bivouac area during a reenactment.

The vehicle is viewed from the left side while in motion. The M24 had a specified top speed of 35 mph, 1 mph less than that of the Light Tank M5.

In the foreground in this view from the left side of the M24 are the hood for the actuating handle for the interior fire extinguisher, and the tow cable and the cable keeper: a twisted piece of steel, welded to the hull. On the engine deck is an equipment pouch, secured in place with leather straps through footman loops. Next to the pouch is the engine-air intake.

The rear part of the engine deck of an M24 is displayed, with a postwar equipment rack present on the rear of the hull. The grille was for expelling air from the engine compartment; on each front corner of the grille, an exhaust tailpipe protrudes.

This photo and the two following ones show the engine compartment of a Light Tank M24 preserved at the Veterans Memorial Museum in Huntsville, Alabama. This view was taken above the engine-air outlet grille, facing forward. The two white ducts are the carburetor air intakes; the carburetors are below the elbows. *Eli Geher, US Veterans Memorial Museum*

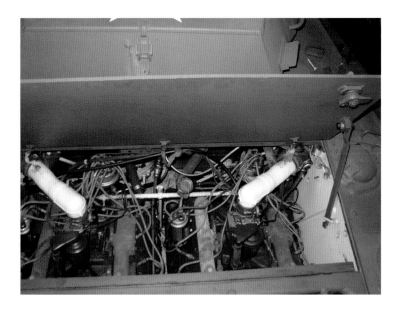

The interior of the open door of the engine compartment is in view; on its right side are a latch and a hold-open brace. At the top of the photo is the storage compartment on the rear of the turret bustle. *Eli Geher, US Veterans Memorial Museum*

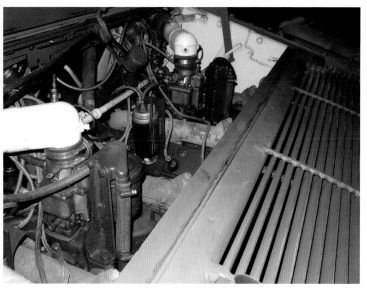

In a view of the engine compartment from the left rear, in the foreground is the Olive Drab–colored crankcase-ventilating air cleaner for the left engine block. The corresponding air cleaner for the right crankcase is in the background. The black-and-aluminum-colored feature between these two air cleaners is the ignition coil for the left engine. *Eli Geher, US Veterans Memorial Museum*

With the driver's hatch door (*left*) swung open on the Mullins M24, part of the interior of the driver's compartment is visible. Note the rubber gasket around the perimeter of the hatch opening, and the cam lock for the hatch door on the opposite side of the hatch, protected by a splash guard welded to the hull. To the right is part of the driver's detachable windshield. *Dave Harper*

The driver's compartment of the Mullins M24 is seen from over the driver's seat. The lever with the knob to the upper left is the interior lock handle for the hatch door. Below the data plates to the left are brackets for storing a .45-caliber submachine gun. Above the instrument panel is a grab handle, and below the instrument panel, on the left final-drive cover, are shifting instructions. To the front of the seat are the steering levers. *Dave Harper*

To the right of the driver's seat are the transfer-unit shift lever and a storage case for periscopes and periscope heads. This case also acted as a guard over the forward driveshaft, to prevent injury to the drivers when the shaft was in motion. *Eli Geher, US Veterans Memorial Museum*

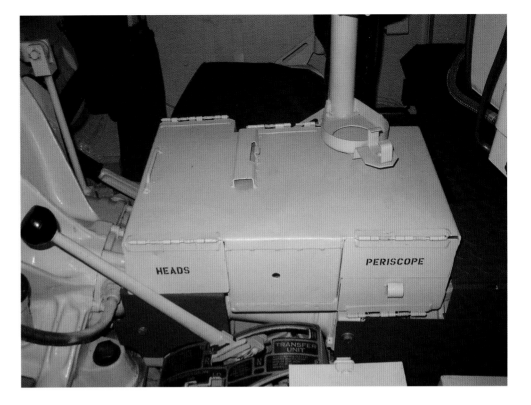

The assistant driver / bow gunner's seat is viewed through the open hatch. A weatherproof gasket and a crash pad surround the hatch opening. To the front of the seat are the assistant driver's steering levers and collector bags for spent machine gun casings and links. *Eli Geher, US Veterans Memorial Museum*

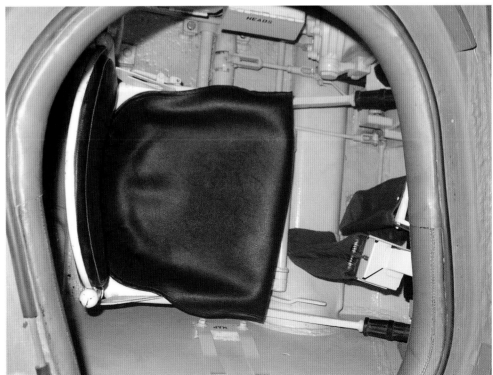

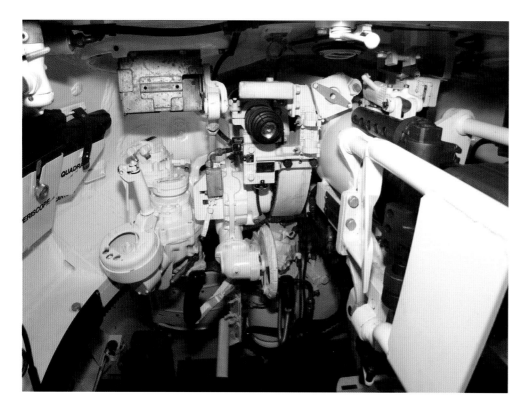

The gunner's station in the left front of the turret of the Mullins M24 is viewed as the gunner would see it. To the left, on the wall of the turret, are a stored M6 periscope and a gunner's quadrant, a portable instrument for measuring the elevation of the main gun, particularly when conducting indirect-fire missions. Mounted on the roof is the gunner's Periscope Mount M66, to the right of which is the gunner's telescopic sight (in World War II, the Telescope M71K). Below that periscope is the manual traverse control, and below the sight are the hydraulic-powered traverse control and elevating handwheel. To the right is the 75 mm Gun M6 in Mount M64, with its recoil guard. *Dave Harper*

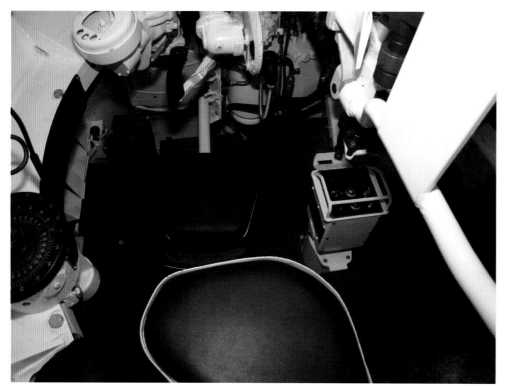

Looking down and forward from the vehicle commander's station, in the foreground is the commander's seat, to the front of which is the gunner's seat. To the left is the Azimuth Indicator M21, a precision instrument used in setting the azimuth, or traverse, of the main gun when conducting indirect fire: that is, targets not in the gunner's line of sight. The white box on the floor contains the turret controls, including those for the gun stabilizer, the turret traversing motor, and the gun master switch. *Dave Harper*

This is a loader's-eye view of the right side of the 75 mm gun breech. The breech block slid to the left when opened; here, it is closed. The white cylinder with the cable and elbow routed into it is the firing solenoid. The white tube at the top is part of the recoil guard. *Chris Hughes*

The Combination Gun Mount M64 is viewed from the loader's perspective. The main part of the mount seen here is the Olive Drab recoil cylinder, which contains a concentric hydrospring mechanism, inside which is situated the gun barrel. The concentric recoil cylinder saved space by eliminating the external recoil cylinders normally used on tank guns in World War II. On the right side of the recoil cylinder are the right trunnion and its mounting bracket on the turret. *Chris Hughes*

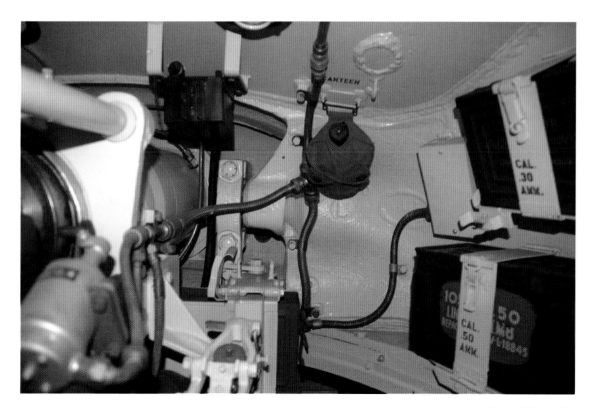

This is another loader's-eye view, showing the 75 mm gun and combination mount to the left and stored ammunition boxes on the turret wall to the right. The mount for the .30-caliber coaxial machine gun and its ammunition box is at the lower center. A canteen is stored on the roof.

CHAPTER 2
Field Use

The first consignment of M24s to arrive in northwestern Europe landed at Cherbourg, France, in early December 1944 and were forwarded to the 744th Tank Battalion, 9th US Army. Five M24s, presumably serving with the 744th, are lined up near Kornelimünster, in Aachen District, Germany, on December 26, 1944. Note the folded-down windshields to the fronts of the driver's hatches. *National Archives*

Twenty M24 tanks were sent to Europe in late 1944. Initially, the Army planned to reequip the 744th Tank Battalion with these tanks. Coincidental with the arrival of the tanks, the German army launched their offensive that would come to be known as the Battle of the Bulge. In the ensuing confusion, two of the twenty M24s were mistakenly delivered to the 740th Tank Battalion, which had recently arrived without any tanks of any kind. The unit immediately put the Chaffees into service, and into combat. The remaining eighteen tanks were delivered to the 744th on Christmas Eve.

The Army next began issuing Chaffees to cavalry reconnaissance squadrons, and once those units were reequipped with the new tanks, then the M24s began to replace Stuarts within armored divisions.

The tanks saw combat in the Ardennes-Alsace, Rhineland, and central Europe. Additionally, the 1st Armored Division's 81st Cavalry Reconnaissance Squadron used the tanks in Italy.

Although the Marine Corps received ten Chaffees for testing, they ultimately rejected the vehicle. However, the Soviets received two examples, and the British received 289 of the vehicles.

After World War II, the Chaffee completely replaced the Stuart in US service and was used by occupation troops in Japan, Austria, and Germany. They were among the first tanks to see combat when the Korean War broke out in 1950. There, the light tanks were outmatched by the Soviet-supplied T-34s operated by the Communists, a situation compounded by the poor maintenance that many of the tanks had received while on occupation duty in Japan.

By 1953, the M24 was being replaced by the M41 Walker Bulldog in US service. Becoming surplus, the tanks were supplied to Allied nations, chief of which was France, which received 1,254 of the tanks, some of which were subsequently used in Indochina, including famously at the Battle of Dien Bien Phu in 1954. Additionally, South Vietnam received 137 tanks directly from the United States. Belgium, Italy, Norway, and Turkey were among the twenty-eight nations that were furnished the vehicles.

The 13th Tank Battalion was an early user of the Light Tank M24. Here, a column of M24s from Company D of that battalion are stopped in a village in Italy to refuel during the winter of 1944–45. The tankers are filling the fuel tanks by using captured German Jerrycans. *Patton Museum*

An M24 from Company D, 740th Tank Battalion, in Nonceveux, Belgium, has been whitewashed to better blend in with the snowy terrain. The photo was taken on January 19, 1945. At the time, this battalion was attached to the 82nd Airborne Division. Note the US 5-gallon liquid containers lying on the fenders, the driver's detachable windshield (the glass of which is cracked), and the dust cover over the bow machine gun. *National Archives*

Soldiers from Company D, 740th Tank Battalion, are gathered around an M24, likely the same one in the preceding photo, in Nonceveux, Belgium. The whitewash camouflage extended even to the ammunition box on the .50-caliber machine gun mount. *Patton Museum*

The crew of "Ally Oop III" had made no effort to camouflage their M24 for wintertime operations. The vehicle and crew appear in this posed photo in Germany in January 1945. Note the M6 periscope on the driver's hatch door. *National Archives*

Lieutenant Tom Munford, from an unidentified tank battalion, is standing on the hull of an M24, giving the troops below, from the 9th Infantry Division, a familiarization lecture on the new tank in an occupied town in the western part of Germany on January 21, 1945. Such instruction was important for US troops in areas where M24s were operating, since these new tanks with their unfamiliar shapes were unfamiliar to many GIs. *National Archives*

Crewmen of a Light Tank 24 from the 18th Cavalry Reconnaissance Squadron, 14th Cavalry Group, take a break on their whitewashed vehicle in Petit Tiers, France, in February 1945. They have placed a canvas cover over the end of the 75 mm gun to keep out mud and foreign objects. The skirts have been removed from the fenders, leaving three tapered mounting brackets in view. A section of wooden log has been placed on the front of the glacis as a retainer for packs and equipment. *National Archives*

An M24, numbered "3" on the turret, and crew from the 81st Reconnaissance Squadron, 1st Armored Division, pause during the advance through a war-ravaged village south of Bologna, Italy, in early 1945. A bracket has been added to the glacis to hold two 5-gallon liquid containers. Hanging from the turret is a Thompson submachine gun with the stock removed and an extra clip of ammo taped on. *Patton Museum*

Infantrymen of the 8th Armored Division, US 9th Army, maneuver between two M24s, one of which has been hit and is smoldering, at Rhineberg, Germany, on March 6, 1945. On the rears of the hulls of both tanks, the original tarpaulin bins have been removed and new, larger storage bins have been installed. *National Archives*

Troops of the 35th Infantry Regiment are passing a Light Tank M24 of the 8th Armored Division during the advance from Rhineberg to Lindforth, Germany, on March 6, 1945. A close inspection of the original photograph reveals that in addition to the standard .50-caliber machine gun, a Browning M1919 .30-caliber machine gun has been mounted on the right side of the turret roof. *National Archives*

With turret traversed to the rear, an M24 from the 43rd Cavalry Reconnaissance Squadron, 26th Division, is negotiating a treadway bridge next to a destroyed bridge over the Saar River on March 13, 1945. Marked on the bow are "CVC 1376" and "P 3-10-45"; the latter may be an indication that (Prestone) antifreeze was added to the coolant system on March 10, 1945. *National Archives*

Two Landing Craft, Mechanized (LCMs), are delivering Light Tanks M24 to shore during one of the Rhine River crossings in Germany. The tank on the right, marked "D-5" on the mantlet, is equipped with sandbag armor, for improved protection against antitank projectiles, on the glacis, turret sides, and fenders. *Patton Museum*

M24s from the 30th Division, US 9th Army, are advancing along a road outside Holthausen, Germany, on March 25, 1945. The two nearest vehicles have field-fabricated storage racks made of angle irons on the bows; the rack on the lead vehicle is holding in place two 5-gallon liquid containers and four M1 helmets stored on the glacis. *National Archives*

An M24 and infantrymen from the 30th Division are engaged in a firefight with enemy forces during the advance on March 25, 1945. The turret is providing cover for the GIs on the engine deck. *National Archives*

A storage rack made of angle irons and wood similar to those seen in the photo of M24s near Holthausen, Germany, on March 25, 1945, is present on another M24 from the 30th Division, photographed the following day outside Wesel, Germany. Arranged behind this rack and on the fenders are sandbags, with camouflage netting stretched over the sandbags on the glacis. The nickname "ABE" is painted on the turret. The troops are from 1st Battalion, 120th Infantry. *National Archives*

Civilians look on as an M24 from Company D, 27th Tank Battalion, 20th Armored Division, Seventh Army, advances into Munich on the date that city was captured, March 30, 1945. Prepared for further enemy resistance, the crewmen are wearing their M1 helmets and are situated low in their hatches. *National Archives*

Two infantrymen, flanking a vehicle crewman manning the .50-caliber machine gun, share a ride on an M24 during the 20th Armored Division's approach to Salzburg, Austria, on May 4, 1945. In the field to the left are two recently knocked-out German tanks. *National Archives*

Residents of Pilsen, Czechoslovakia, turn out in native dress to greet elements of the US 3rd Army entering the city on June 15, 1945. The two M24s have a modified antiaircraft-weapon arrangement, with the tripods moved to the fronts of the cupolas. *National Archives*

Members of the 6th Cavalry Reconnaissance Squadron, 102nd Infantry Division, are practicing some "spit and polish" on their M24 at Coburg, Germany, in preparation for entering Berlin, on July 7, 1945. Tech Sgt. Melvin Kracke, *right*, is getting ready to spray some Olive Drab paint on the glacis, while Tech 5th Class Myron Conley and a mascot look on. A good view is offered of the dust cover for the bow machine gun. *National Archives*

After the German surrender, the US Army prepared to move many of its vehicles and troops to the Pacific for the expected invasion of Japan. Marseilles, France, was a key port of origin for much of this traffic. Here, an M24 is being hoisted to a Liberty ship at Marseilles on August 1, 1945. A large wooden crate of equipment and parts is mounted on the tank's fender. *National Archives*

On the first day of the
Nuremberg Trials of German war
criminals, November 20, 1945, an
M24 crew is on guard outside
the entrance to the trail venue,
the Palace of Justice, ready to
react should civil disorder break
out. *National Archives*

In a vintage color photo of the
Palace of Justice in Nuremberg,
an M24 tank is positioned outside
the main gate. Unit markings are
present on the rear of the hull but
are not legible. *National Archives*

Members of an M24 crew of a tank section of a reconnaissance platoon in the 3rd Cavalry stand for review by their tank in October 20, 1949. The on-vehicle equipment is arranged on platforms for inspection. *3ACR Museum*

In a companion image to the preceding one, on-vehicle equipment for an M24 with Reconnaissance Troop, 1st Squadron, 3rd Cavalry, arranged for inspection at Fort Meade, Maryland, in 1949, includes machine guns, spare barrels, ammo boxes, pioneer tools and hand tools, and accessories. To the upper right are intercom sets and a radio. *3ACR Museum*

Two M24s from Troop B, 3rd Cavalry, are on review at Fort Meade, Maryland, in 1949. The first tank carries a guidon on a staff. On the turret is painted "BRAVE RIFLE," a reference to the regiment's nickname, "Brave Rifles." *3ACR Museum*

A Light Tank M24 has been loaded onto a "Dragon Wagon" Tank Transporter M25 of the 52nd Ordnance Battalion during Exercise Mars in the US Zone in Austria on March 15, 1950. *National Archives*

The same M24 shown in the preceding photo, registration number 30112723, is preparing to debark from the Semitrailer M15 component of the Tank Transporter M25. This tank has the infantry telephone box on the right rear of the hull. *National Archives*

Curious Austrian civilians look on as Light Tank M24, registration number 30112723, is about to roll off the ramps on the rear of the Semitrailer M15 during Operation Mars on March 15, 1950. *National Archives*

The Light Tank M24 saw extensive service in the Korean War, and, in fact, numbers of these tanks were already positioned, along with their crews, in Korea before the war broke out. Here, members of the 31st Regimental Combat Team conduct a training exercise in Korea in late March 1950, three months before the start of the war. *Patton Museum*

During the early days of the Korean War, in the summer of 1950, an M24 patrols a dusty stretch of road in Korea. A machine gun with a dust cover over it is mounted on the turret to the front of the cupola. *Patton Museum*

Still equipped with the original T72 steel tracks from World War II, an M24 rolls past waving civilians in Korea on July 8, 1950, during the second week of the war in that country. *National Archives*

In a photo taken on the same date as the preceding one, and apparently at the same unidentified location in Korea, an M24 advances along a muddy road in a village. Covers are installed over the 75 mm gun muzzle, the bow machine gun, and the driver's lowered windshield. *National Archives*

A crewman in the cupola of an M24 keeps watch over the sky in Korea on July 8, 1950. Evergreen boughs have been amply heaped on the vehicle for camouflage. *National Archives*

A Light Tank M24 proceeds along a raised road alongside a rice paddy in Korea on July 8, 1950. Many of the M24s in Korea in the earliest days of the war had been quickly shipped there from Japan. The first engagement between M24s and Communist armor would be two days after this photo was taken. *Patton Museum*

On July 9, 1950, crewmen of a dug-in M24 await orders in Korea. If necessary, the tank could quickly drive forward and out of the entrenchment. Note the extra radio antenna mounted on what formerly was the smoke-grenade mortar housing, on the right front of the turret roof. *National Archives*

Taken on July 10, 1950, this photo reportedly shows one of the M24s that on the morning of that date fought the first tank engagement of the Korean War, near Chonui. The M24s in that fight were from Company A, 78th Heavy Tank Battalion, and the Tank Platoon of the 24th Reconnaissance Company. The M24s did not fare well against the Soviet-built T-34-85 tanks, armed with very potent 85 mm main guns. *National Archives*

This is said to be a photograph of one of the M24s that participated in the first tank engagement in the Korean War, taken on the day of that fight. *National Archives*

This M24, with the nickname "REBEL'S ROOST" on the turret, was one of those that fought in the first engagement with Communist Korean armor on July 10, 1950. The vehicle, shown here with its crew, was assigned to the Tank Platoon, 24th Reconnaissance Company, 24th Infantry Division. Note the towel and T-shirts hung out to dry on the 75 mm gun, the dismounted .30-caliber machine gun on the glacis, and the bore-cleaning staff leaning against the bow. *Patton Museum*

Crewmen of "REBEL'S ROOST" are cleaning the .30-caliber machine gun and stowing gear after the engagement on July 10, 1950. On the fenders are the unit markings "24 X" and "24-R 21." Another M24 is in the background. *National Archives*

On July 13, 1950, a crewman is scanning Communist positions in the distance with binoculars, while sitting on an M24 positioned in an entrenchment along the Kum River dike in Korea. The crew has laid a tarpaulin over the front of the turret and a shirt or jacket over the .50-caliber machine gun for camouflage. *National Archives*

Crewmen from the M24 nicknamed "REBEL'S ROOST," with the Tank Platoon, 24th Reconnaissance Company, are replenishing 75 mm ammunition during a lull in the action on July 19, 1950. It was on this date that the 24th Reconnaissance Company lost its first tank in battle. *National Archives*

Members of the crew of a Light Tank M24 with the 25th Infantry Division confer with a Korean local while parked on a sandy plain near a repaired bridge over a river on July 24, 1950. *National Archives*

A Light Tank M24 from the 25th Reconnaissance Company has been positioned under a tree, no doubt for camouflage purposes, in Korea on July 24, 1950. Field packs are stored on the left side of the turret, and a bedroll with an M1 helmet on top of it is on the right fender. *National Archives*

An M24 and crew are in a dug-in overwatch position somewhere on the Korean Peninsula on July 24, 1950. Standing next to the turret is a Korean wearing what appears to be civilian clothes and a hat or helmet with foliage on it for camouflage. *National Archives*

The crew of this Light Tank M24 from the 79th Heavy Tank Battalion, 25th Infantry Division, have placed the vehicle in a concealed firing position outside Hamchang, Korea, on July 24, 1950. All too often in the early days of the Korean War, M24s were called on to sacrifice their chief virtues, speed and maneuverability, for use as static-defensive fire platforms. *National Archives*

Members of the crew of an M24 assigned to the 25th Reconnaissance Squadron, 25th Infantry Division, pose for their photograph along a road in Korea on July 25, 1950. The sign on the post next to the tree, possibly painted by a local Korean with some knowledge of English, reads, "TANGS [right pointing arrow] / GO.THIS.WAY." *National Archives*

Microphone in hand and headphones on, a crewman, likely the vehicle commander, of a Light Tank M24 is communicating by radio during an action in Korea on July 26, 1950. In the right foreground is a vane sight, which allowed the commander, sighting through the front vision block on the cupola, to quickly align the turret on a target.
National Archives

GIs are handing up a resupply of 75 mm ammunition to a crewman on an M24 from the 25th Reconnaissance Company at a site 7 miles north of Masan, Korea, on August 10, 1950. The original lightweight expanded-steel mesh grille on the tarpaulin bin on the rear of the hull has been replaced by a heavier-duty sheet metal with oblong lightening holes on it. *National Archives*

In a posed photo, crewmen of a Light Tank M24 from the 24th Reconnaissance Squadron, 24th Infantry Division, are at the ready with small arms while guarding an intersection in Korea on August 17, 1950. The men are Pfc. Rudolph Dotts, sitting on the ground; Pvt. Maynard Linaweaver, sitting on the driver's hatch; and Pfc. Hugh Goodwin, vehicle commander, in the cupola. Although the sand skirts have been removed from the fender, one of the tapered brackets for supporting the skirt is still in place. *National Archives*

An M24 of the 24th Infantry Division has been embarked on a pontoon raft for ferrying across the Nakdong River, Korea, during an offensive against Communist forces on September 20, 1950. Equipment racks, fabricated apparently from welded rods, have been installed on the fenders and are full of rations boxes, bedrolls, and other gear. *US Army Engineer School History Office*

The Light Tank M24 formed part of the armored force stationed in West Germany during the early Cold War era. Here, two mechanics from garrison maintenance are in a grease pit, lubricating the bogie wheels of M24 no. 73 from Headquarters, 63rd Tank Battalion, at Mannheim, West Germany, on March 20, 1951. On the differential-access door on the glacis is artwork: a skull with an ax through it, below which is "RCN" (reconnaissance) over a lightning bolt. *National Archives*

After World War II, the Free Territory of Trieste was formed along the Adriatic coast, comprising an area contested by the Italians and the Yugoslavians. A peacekeeping force sent there included the TRUST Force ("TRieste US Troops"), which included the 351st Infantry. Here, an M24 crew from that regiment pauses during a three-day field problem in the Free Territory of Trieste on August 15, 1951. *National Archives*

During the Operation Totem Pole maneuvers in Alaska on August 25, 1951, M24 crewmen are preparing their vehicle for action. This tank is equipped with the T85E1 rubber-shoed, double-pin tracks. *National Archives*

A Light Tank M24 from the 3rd Cavalry and attached to the Aggressor Force pauses while its vehicle commander determines his next objective during the first week of Exercise Southern Pine, a joint Army–Air Force maneuver in North Carolina in August 1951. A large, heavily weathered "BRAVE RIFLES" insignia of the 3rd Cavalry is on the glacis. *National Archives*

Two soldiers from the 1st Armored Division, with only their helmets visible above the ground, are preparing to duck down into foxholes as an M24 from the 81st Reconnaissance Battalion is about to roll over them. This exercise was intended to accustom troops to coping with an armored onslaught. *National Archives*

Col. E. M. Culligan, *right*, from the US 7th Army, two Italian officers, and US tank crewman are gathered on a Light Tank M24, registration number 30121114, during Field Training Exercise '51 (FTX-1). The reference to "Gen. Warringa" is not clear. *National Archives*

On January 21, 1952, members of an M24 crew from Company C, 4th Reconnaissance Battalion, pause during Exercise Snowshoe, a seven-day winter-training exercise involving US Forces in Austria (USFA). The site was near Neumark. Note the canvas foul-weather hood attached to the lowered windshield to the front of the driver's hatch, and the pedestal-mounted .50-caliber machine gun to the front of the cupola. *National Archives*

During Exercise Long Horn, a joint Army–Air Force maneuver at Fort Hood, Texas, on March 22, 1952, the crew of this Light Tank M24 decorated the bow of their vehicle with, appropriately enough, a pair of genuine Texas longhorns, measuring over 7 feet wide. Covers are installed over the service headlights. *National Archives*

The Butzbach Ordnance Depot, in Butzbach, West Germany, rebuilt this Light Tank M24 for use as a target during firing practice. As photographed on March 5, 1952, the tank had armored skirts on the sides of the hull to protect the tracks and suspension. Stronger fender braces were installed to support the weight of the skirts. The 75 mm gun and the bow machine gun were removed and the opening was covered with armor. Other openings on the tank that were susceptible to projectiles also were covered. The drivers' periscopes received armored enclosures. *National Archives*

At Shop No. 2 at the Butzbach Ordnance Depot, a German worker is removing a sprocket assembly from the chassis of an M24 being rebuilt while a supervisor looks on in the background, on October 14, 1953. The guns and the suspension have been removed from the tank. An excellent view is available of the exterior part of the left final-drive assembly and the upper front of the controlled differential. A rail for storing crew equipment had been welded to the side of the turret. Two more M24s are in the background.
National Archives

An M24, registration number 30112603, is being sprayed clean in an ordnance facility, presumably the one at Butzbach, West Germany. Located near Frankfurt, the Butzbach Ordnance Depot was established by US Army Ordnance in late March 1945, using two existing factory facilities. *National Archives*

Newly rebuilt Light Tanks M24 are lined up at the Butzbach Ordnance Depot on October 14, 1953, ready for shipment to their units. The first vehicle has its registration number on the differential-access door: 30121667. All vehicles have large crates containing vehicular equipment and parts secured to their engine decks. The T85E1 tracks have been installed, along with the requisite thirteen-tooth sprocket assemblies. *National Archives*

After the armistice bringing a cessation to combat in the Korean War, some M24s continued to serve in that theater. Shown here, with turret traversed to the rear and parked under a cover of camouflage netting and scrim, is an M24 from the 40th Reconnaissance Company, 40th US Infantry Division, on the southern side of the Demilitarized Zone on December 12, 1953. A large number "25" is painted on the side of the turret. *National Archives*

By 1952, with Japan soon to formally establish its Self-Defense Forces, the United States began supplying M24s to that country. In this photo, dated late December 1953, a column of M24s in Japanese service are proceeding along a road on the island of Honshu during a military exercise. Camouflage netting has been stretched over the glacis and the mantlet of at least the first two tanks. *Library of Congress*

The French employed the Light Tank M24 in their ill-fated postwar effort to regain control of their colony of French Indochina. In this photo, members of *2e Compagnie de Réparation d'Engins Blindés de la Légion Étrangère* (2nd Company of Armored Engine Repair of the Foreign Legion) are preparing for reassembly several M24s from *1er Régiment de Chasseurs á Cheval* (1st Cavalry Regiment) that had been transported, disassembled, by air transport to the base at Dien Bien Phu. *ECPAD*

French mechanics are working to reassemble a turretless M24 at Dien Bien Phu. These tanks, numbering ten in all, were reassembled from December 25, 1953, until January 15, 1954. At Dien Bien Phu, the French referred to the M24s by the nickname "Bisons." *ECPAD*

An M24 in French service is fording a rice paddy at Muong Thanh field, Dien Bien Phu, in early 1954. A storage box is attached with wires to the differential-access door; on the lower front of the hull is a bridge classification sign with the number "18." *Patton Museum*

During the 1954 Battle of Dien Bien Phu, a column of M24s is returning fire while crossing a field. On the lead tank, an insignia and the number "2" are visible on the side of the turret. After the defeat of the French at Dien Bien Phu, an M24 captured by the Viet Minh remained on display at the site of that battle. *ECPAD*

As the 1950s progressed, use of the Light Tank M24 in the US armed forces was restricted to some National Guard units. Here, kids are enjoying a chance to explore an M24 on exhibit during Armed Forces Day at Fort Richardson, Alaska, on May 19, 1954. On the right mudguard are markings for the 12th Tank Company, and painted on the mantlet is the nickname of that unit, "THE DIRTY DOZEN." *National Archives*

Several M24s are lined up in a clearing in Alaska during a training exercise in 1954. Marked on the turret is a white triangle, above which is the nickname "CLEO." On the upper hull is the registration number, 30139138. Among other gear, a broom is wedged in next to the turret bustle. Note the rail on the side of the turret, for storing field packs and similar gear, welded between the lifting eye and the shield for the .50-caliber machine gun when stored. *National Archives*

In the 1950s, the United States began supplying military equipment to the Republic of Vietnam to counter Communist advances following the defeat and withdrawal of the French. Eventually, US deliveries of the Light Tank M24 to the Vietnamese totaled 137. This example was photographed at the 80th Ordnance Base Depot, at Tan Son Nhut, Vietnam, on January 10, 1967. *National Archives*

The same M24 depicted in the preceding photo is viewed from another angle at Tan Son Nhut on January 10, 1067. Stenciled in small letters on the side of the turret is "M.D.A.P.," the acronym for the Military Defense Assistance Program, under the auspices of which war materiel and assistance were furnished to America's allies. *National Archives*

Entering combat in the final year of World War II, the Light Tank M24 had many advantages, especially in firepower, over its predecessors, including the Light Tank M5A1, but lacked sufficient firepower to cope with the enemy armor encountered in the early weeks and months of the Korean War. Nevertheless, its speed, mobility, maneuverability, reliability, low profile, and, against the right enemy equipment, its firepower, endeared it to its crews in several wars and conflicts.